PET OWNER'S GUIDE TO THE
LURCHER

Jason Framingham

RINGPRESS

DEDICATION

To my wife, Jenny, for her everlasting patience (and for nagging me to get on with it).
To my brother, Marc, for those much-needed days off fishing.

ACKNOWLEDGEMENTS

To Liz and Jim Colley, and all the members of the Crossbreed and Mongrel Club;
Fiona Redworth of Redlands Dog Training; and Sue Clayton of Torksey Waifs and
Strays, for all the advice they have given me. Many thanks to Evesham Lurcher and
Greyhound Rescue for providing several dogs to photograph.

ABOUT THE AUTHOR

Jason Framingham lives in Lincolnshire with
his wife, two Lurchers, two Terrier crosses, an
elderly Whippet and two cats! His love of
Lurchers began while he was still a child, and
he eventually acquired one of his own.

Not intending to work his Lurcher, Jason
sought alternative ways of keeping his dog's
active mind occupied. This led to a love of
Agility, Obedience and racing, in which Jason
and his wife regularly participate with their dogs.
Jason's Lurchers have also appeared in several
television and newspaper commercials.

Much of Jason's spare time is spent promoting
Lurchers and other crossbred dogs. He sits on
the Crossbreed and Mongrel Club and helps his
wife manage the club's telephone helplines,
giving advice to dog owners everywhere.

Published by Ringpress Books,
A Division of INTERPET LTD,
Vincent Lane, Dorking, Surrey, RH4 3YX

First published 2001
© Interpet Publishing. All rights reserved

Designed by: Sara Howell

ISBN 13   978 1 86054 193 3
ISBN 10   1 86054 193 3

Printed and bound in Hong Kong through Printworks International Ltd.

CONTENTS

1 *Introducing The Lurcher*

What is a Lurcher? A Lurcher is a crossbreed of dog that contains at least one sighthound in its ancestry (see Chapter Two). To date, the Lurcher has not yet achieved official recognition by canine societies such as national kennel clubs. However, despite its lack of breed recognition, the Lurcher is an extremely popular type of dog.

PORTRAIT OF A LURCHER

"Under a poacher's moon the dogs stand, muscles tense, ears held high, nostrils flaring to catch the scent... with natural instinct flowing through their veins, and the muted calls of their masters' voices growing ever distant behind them, they are on the chase..."

As noble as the above description is, a far more likely scenario would be "their master's voice growing ever distant behind them as they leg it from the kitchen to the garden to eat the pork chop which they have just stolen from the kitchen table!".

The picture we have of the Lurcher has been endlessly romanticised, and usually describes a dog which is fleet of foot, sharp of mind, and traditionally belongs to the local poacher. While this picture is certainly appealing, it provides little insight into the nature of these remarkable dogs.

A HISTORY OF THE LURCHER

The exact history of the Lurcher is not known, and what *is* known is widely disputed. Nevertheless, there is evidence to place the Lurcher in Britain as far back as the 11th century. At this time Greyhound coursing was the sport of noblemen. Peasants were only permitted to own running dogs on condition that the dog had been 'hobbled'. This practice required the animal's foot to be broken, or the rear leg to be amputated. It was introduced to prevent peasants

Fast, agile and skilful, the Lurcher was highly valued as a companion of poachers.

using dogs to poach livestock belonging to nobles. Although the hobbling laws were extreme, they were obeyed. The punishment for breaking the rules was hanging.

The Lurcher only really became commonplace in the early 18th century. The first intentionally-bred Lurcher crosses were long-legged Collie types, with the most likely crossing being between Smithfield Collies (similar to the Border Collies of today, except larger and longer-legged) and Greyhounds. The dogs were probably bred by drovers, not only for herding, but also to hunt for food while flocks

of livestock were transported all over the country. Possibly originating in the East Anglian counties of England, these types of dogs are still known as Norfolk Lurchers.

During the latter part of the 18th and the first half of the 19th centuries, the Lurcher's role as the poaching dog came into being. The speed, agility and skill of these dogs allowed their owners to escape detection when poaching – an extremely valuable skill, since poaching was punishable by flogging, deportation, or, on very rare occasions, hanging.

In the latter part of the 19th century, the Retriever-Greyhound cross became popular with the warreners of large country estates. These men were employed to manage the rabbit populations, and used Lurchers, alongside ferrets, to either run the warrens as a viable food source, or to cull the rabbits in order to protect valuable crops. The Lurchers were very successful at chasing and catching the rabbits, and were also able to retrieve other varieties of poached game. Such trophies were usually retrieved from water, dead, although live quarry was taken from land. The input of the Retriever in Lurcher breeding also meant that the resulting crosses were able to hunt by scent as well as sight – a relatively new concept in Lurcher breeding – which increased the dog's potential for other uses.

THE LURCHER IN WARTIME

The Lurcher's reputation for being a fast, intelligent and courageous dog grew during the early part of the 20th century. By the time World War I had broken out, the

The introduction of Retriever blood increased the Lurcher's range of skills.

military had taken an interest in the use of Lurchers for the war effort. After field-testing the dogs, army officials were so impressed that they put Lurchers to immediate use as messenger dogs on the front lines in France.

Meanwhile, in Britain, rationing was in full force. The popularity of the Lurcher rose when the dog's skill at hunting to provide fresh meat for the table was realised. Lurchers became a valuable asset, and many people were prepared to pay a lot of money to acquire one.

LURCHERS AND GYPSIES

Gypsies, although reputed to have had a long association with the Lurcher, only became involved with the breed during the years immediately after the Great War. The nomadic lifestyle, which took the gypsies all over the world, made them realise that each geographical area had its own requirements. The gypsies responded by selectively breeding Lurchers to suit the various demands.

For example, in Britain, where the Lurcher-type crossbreed originated, a Deerhound cross was especially favoured in Scotland. The Greyhound's agility and speed, coupled with the Deerhound's

hardiness and endurance, were ideally suited to the terrain. However, in Northumberland and Yorkshire, the Bedlington cross was favoured. These dogs were not bred with Greyhounds but with Whippets, producing a smaller dog who was agile enough to 'turn on a tanner' and had the stamina to work for hours in the cold and wet.

THREAT OF MYXOMATOSIS

The growth of the Lurcher's popularity continued unchecked until the 1950s. By this time, the Lurcher was bred almost exclusively for catching rabbits. When myxomatosis struck the UK, not only was the rabbit population decimated (it is estimated that the disease left as few as five million rabbits in the whole of Britain), but the future of the Lurcher was also under threat.

COURSING

While some people still bred and kept Lurchers for their food-providing abilities, from the late 1950s onwards, the dogs were bred primarily for coursing hares. An active interest in the breeding of Lurchers followed, as sleeker, more agile and faster dogs became sought after. The Lurchers

When the Lurcher was crossed with a Saluki, it produced a faster, finer dog.

produced at this time, such as the Saluki cross, bore little resemblance to the sturdier Collie-type crosses of the previous centuries.

THE LURCHER TODAY

With the advent of selective breeding in the world of hare-coursing, the characteristic Lurcher became a sleek and elegant creature. This effect did not go unnoticed and Lurchers began to be exhibited at dog shows.

The first Lurcher show was held in the early 1970s in Berkshire, and, for the first time in the history of the breed, the dogs were judged on aesthetic grounds rather than on their physical prowess in the field.

Similar shows began to spring up all over the country, and, over time, Obedience, Agility and Racing shows were included.

Today's Lurcher is a highly adaptable animal. It is still happy

Lurchers are now regularly exhibited at dog shows.

to hunt for rabbits under a poacher's moon, but it is equally at home in the club show ring, on the race track, or occupying the sofa as a much-loved family pet.

MYSTERY NAME

The origin of the name 'Lurcher' is a highly controversial issue. Everyone who knows something about the breed is likely to have a different theory, and nearly all of the arguments are equally persuasive. It is for the reader to decide which one seems the most plausible.

THE THIEF

The Romany word for thief is *Lur.* Given the association between the Romany people and Lurchers, it is quite plausible that the modern name of Lurcher is a derivation from the Romany language.

Another possibility is that *Lur*, combined with the word *cur*, forms the phrase *Lur-cur*, meaning 'thieving mongrel'. The Lurcher's original use as a poaching animal would support this theory. Also, anyone who has owned a Lurcher will testify that the phrase 'thieving mongrel' has escaped their lips on numerous occasions when lunch has disappeared down the garden in the jaws of the dog!

THE FRENCH ARISTOCRAT

The French for hunting dog is *le chasseur*. French was one of the main languages among the Norman-British upper classes from the late 11th century onwards. It is highly likely that *le chasseur* evolved over time, with the help of some strong regional accents, into 'Lurcher', the modern form we use today.

THE HUNTER

During the early development of the breed, there were two types of hunting dog, Tumblers and Lurchers. Each type took its name from its style of hunting.

Tumblers captured their prey by deliberately colliding with it. The impact stunned the prey, which tumbled – hence the name – to the ground, upon which the dog would retrieve the animal and return it to its owner. This method of hunting became unpopular when the dogs suffered injuries from high-impact collisions or from missing the prey entirely and colliding with the ground.

Lurchers acquired their name from the characteristic lurch they made shortly before catching their prey. The Lurcher chased his quarry by forcing it to turn in a series of zig-zag manoeuvres. This continued until the Lurcher was in a position to make a final 'lurch' and seize his victim. This type of chase caused little damage to the Lurcher, who, because he sustained fewer injuries, soon became more popular than the Tumbler.

2 Types Of Lurcher

Consisting of crossbreeds, the Lurcher group is very diverse, but there are three main categories.

- Sighthound x sighthound crosses
- Sighthound x terrier crosses
- Sighthound x herding-dog crosses.

The dominant characteristics of each dog determine which group he will be placed in. For example, an Irish Wolfhound cross may contain up to six different breeds of dog in his genetic make-up, but if he was overwhelmingly Wolfhound-like in appearance, he would be known as a Wolfhound Lurcher. In short, your Lurcher will adopt the name of whichever breed he most closely resembles.

SIGHTHOUND CROSSES
There are two types of hound: sighthounds and scenthounds. Sighthounds, who have made the most significant genetic contribution to the Lurcher's gene pool, are the sleeker and more agile dogs of the hound group, and include Greyhounds, Whippets Deerhounds and Wolfhounds, as well as more exotic members such as the Sloughi.

Technically speaking, dogs who are the product of a mating between one sighthound and another are not Lurchers. Instead, these animals are officially known as 'Long Dogs'. This name is rarely used today, however, and most running-dog crosses are known colloquially as Lurchers.

DEERHOUND LURCHER
The Deerhound Lurcher is an extremely pretty dog. He usually has a rough coat of varying shades of grey, sometimes with white flashes on the chest and paws. There is also a brindle variety, but this is not as common. This Lurcher type is very large, especially in the first and second generation crosses.

The Deerhound Lurcher is a big dog with lots of energy.

The Deerhound cross is not the easiest dog to train, having a seemingly inexhaustible amount of energy, and a somewhat limited intellect! The cross requires an experienced, patient, and energetic owner, and training needs to be repetitive, fun and constant. Collie breeds have been mated to the Deerhound cross in an attempt to improve intelligence and concentration, but success has been limited.

WOLFHOUND LURCHER
The Wolfhound cross is not dissimilar to the Deerhound cross in terms of appearance, both sharing similar grey colouring. Occasionally, a wheaten-coloured Wolfhound cross will appear, and these animals are among the most handsome of dogs. The Wolfhound Lurcher possesses a unique character, and is renowned for his clumsiness, which is probably related to his size and lack of brain power!

The Wolfhound cross is huge in comparison to other Lurchers – three feet high (approximately one metre) is not uncommon. The cross was bred to be a long-distance

The Wolfhound Lurcher is the giant of the Lurcher crosses.

runner, presenting an impressive sight when in motion. However, his size and build are disadvantages when it comes to small-prey coursing, since this crossbreed lacks the necessary acceleration and agility for this pursuit.

BORZOI LURCHER

The Borzoi Lurcher is in high demand, difficult to obtain, and expensive to purchase. He is larger than the average Lurcher, but is dwarfed by the Wolfhound cross. This crossbreed is the beauty of the Lurcher group. He is noble in appearance, has a small, delicate head, fine-boned limbs, and a beautifully silky coat (a nightmare for the person entrusted with keeping it in condition). The Borzoi Lurcher is enjoying increased popularity in the show ring, and is probably best suited to someone who takes pride in constant grooming, and who wants to exhibit their dog at a non-pedigree dog show.

Unfortunately, many are extremely difficult to train – the basic commands, such as Sit and Down, being all that most owners ever achieve. If you want a dog who walks to heel, or has any kind of obedience skills, the Borzoi Lurcher is not the best option.

This Borzoi Lurcher is not showing the characteristic coat, making it one of the rarer crosses to find.

SALUKI LURCHER

The pure-bred Saluki is among the oldest-known breeds of dog, and is famed for his endurance and stamina – characteristics which are instantly recognisable in his Lurcher relative.

The elegant-looking Saluki cross is a common sight in the non-pedigree show ring, where he always seems to do well. He has a

Saluki Lurchers are full of character.

typically long, flat face, larger-than-average ears, and a slight, small-boned skeleton. The crossbreed's coat is soft and silky, and comes in a multitude of colours. Certain examples of the crossbreed are found with the feathering of the pure-bred Saluki.

As with the other sighthound crosses, many Saluki crosses are renowned for their lack of intelligence, although this in no way detracts from their suitability as pets. Of all the sighthound Lurcher crosses, this is one crossbreed with a huge personality, and he makes an endearing and enjoyable companion.

WHIPPET LURCHER

If most sighthound Lurchers are found wanting in the brains department, then the Whippet cross is the exception which proves the rule. A highly intelligent dog, the Whippet has been a long-established favourite among Lurcher breeders. Today's pure-bred Whippets are actually the descendants of Lurchers. After World War II, the Whippet was crossed with the Greyhound and the Bedlington Terrier. Today's Whippets are the product of those breeding programmes.

The Whippet Lurcher gets on especially well with children.

Whippet crosses make ideal pets. They are very good-natured and thrive in the home environment. They bond well with all members of the family and are extremely tolerant of children. As a general rule, most Lurchers with a predominance of Whippet genes have an outstanding ability to learn. This makes them ideal candidates for canine activities such as Agility, Flyball and Obedience.

GREYHOUND LURCHER

The Greyhound, a close relative of the Saluki, is thought to have developed in the Arab states of the Middle East. An ancient breed, a Greyhound-like dog is depicted on the interior walls of the Egyptian pyramids. The Greyhound is also believed to have been the favoured dog of the Celts, who valued the breed's hunting prowess, and its ferocity and courage on the battle-field. This ancient version of the dog would have been much larger than the sighthound x Greyhound cross seen today, however.

The modern Greyhound is best known for his speed, which is why Greyhounds are considered to be a vital component in the genetic make-up of the Lurcher. It is estimated that 90 per cent of all running dog crosses contain a significant amount of Greyhound constituents in their DNA. The Greyhound cross is overwhelmingly like the pure-bred, in character, temperament and appearance. He is mild-mannered and very easy to live with. As with

The Greyhound Lurcher bears a strong resemblance to the pure-bred Greyhound in both appearance and temperament.

true Greyhounds, the coat may come in a wide assortment of colours, but the brindle varieties are especially attractive.

OTHER SIGHTHOUND CROSSES

The above are just a few of the more common types of sighthound crosses. However, there are many more examples, such as the Afghan Hound, the Ibizan Hound, the Sloughi and the Pharaoh Hound.

TERRIER CROSSES

Terriers are normally crossed with Greyhounds or Whippets to produce dogs which are fast on the ground, intelligent, and full of spirit. Terrier crosses tend not to

A Whippet x Jack Russell cross: terrier crosses are often lively and spirited.

be as large as their pastoral or sighthound counterparts.

Various terriers are used in Lurcher breeding programmes, with the long-legged types being the most common. The two breeds which are predominantly used are the Bedlington and Staffordshire Bull Terrier crosses. Other terrier crosses tend to be produced for specialist purposes only.

BEDLINGTON LURCHER

The first Bedlington crosses were created by mating the Bedlington Terrier with the Whippet. The resulting dog was originally used for badger-baiting and fox-hunting. The dog was famed for being able to work in harsh climates, on challenging terrain, and so became a very popular choice of working dog.

By the time of World War I, when fresh meat became scarce, the Bedlington Lurcher was several generations old, and had lost the roach back seen in the first-generation crosses. This gave the dog a better running capacity, and he was found to be a natural at coursing – so solving the problem of food rationing.

The Bedlington cross makes a loyal family pet, but requires consistent and firm training. As a

The Bedlington Lurcher is loyal to his family, but requires firm handling.

legacy of his terrier ancestry, this crossbreed can develop aggressive tendencies if allowed to. The Bedlington cross is striking in appearance, because of his unusual and easily recognised coat. The coat is rather woolly, which can make the dog look like the archetypal scruffy mongrel, though to most people this only adds to his appeal.

STAFFORDSHIRE LURCHER

Traditionally, the Staffordshire Bull Terrier is the second most common choice of terrier cross. He is usually the result of a mating between a Staffie and a Whippet, Greyhound, or even a Deerhound. Distinctive in appearance, the Staffie cross is not the best choice of Lurcher for many people, although his popularity would seem to belie this.

Anyone considering taking on a Staffordshire Lurcher, should be aware of the Staffie's history as a fighting dog. This does not mean that all Staffies are nasty dogs, only that the breed has a propensity towards aggression when roused.

In most cases the Staffie cross is a very tolerant animal, who can be trusted – with supervision – around children. However, for those who wish to own such a Lurcher, it is essential to acquire the puppy at as young an age as possible. Thorough socialisation is a must, as is the owner's obligation to establish superiority over the dog. The Staffie cross must *never* be allowed to think of himself as pack leader. Given the correct training, the Staffie Lurcher should be no more dangerous than any other dog – all of which are capable of being big softies or dangerous brutes according to circumstance.

*Mental stimulation is a must
for the Border Collie Lurcher.*

HERDING-DOG CROSSES

Genes from the various Collie breeds are almost as prevalent in the Lurcher as those of the Greyhound. Although there are numerous reasons for this, the main one is to make the Lurcher more intelligent. In turn, this improves the crossbreed's hunting ability. The main pastoral (herding) crosses are the Border Collie, the Bearded Collie and the German Shepherd Dog.

BORDER COLLIE LURCHER

Popularly held to be the most intelligent of dogs, it is easy to see why the Border Collie has become a fixture in the breeding of Lurchers. Easy to train for Working Trials, Flyball,

Obedience, and Agility, the Border Collie possesses all the attributes which are missing from the sighthounds.

Nearly all Lurchers have Collie genes in their make-up. Indeed, many Lurchers are created by crossing the Greyhound with the Border Collie. Collies are normally used to produce first-generation crosses only. The intelligence and agility produced in the resulting litter is usually so well established that no further contribution is required. Most Lurchers today are many generations removed from their original Collie ancestor, but still retain enhanced mental abilities.

There are very few Lurchers which are distinctively Collie-like in appearance, but almost every individual Lurcher will have elements of the Collie in his appearance, e.g. a Greyhound cross with huge Collie-shaped ears, or a Deerhound cross with perfect Collie markings.

Sighthound x Border Collie crosses make excellent pets, due to the ease with which they can be trained. However, they require not only physical exercise, but mental exercise as well. Canine activities such as Agility and Flyball are perfect for this.

BEARDED COLLIE LURCHER

The Bearded Collie was introduced to Lurcher breeding for exactly the same reason as Border Collies. However, in recent years, the Beardie has fallen out of favour with some Lurcher breeders. This is due to a trend which has seen the Beardie become increasingly popular in the show ring. As a consequence, the Beardie may be better-looking than ever, but sometimes this is at the expense of intelligence and working ability.

GERMAN SHEPHERD LURCHER

The German Shepherd Dog (GSD) cross was bred mainly for the pursuit of foxes. These dogs have a great deal in common with their pure-bred ancestors, both in terms of appearance and personality. The only difference between the pure-bred GSD and his Lurcher cousin is that the latter tends to have a slightly higher back and longer legs. The GSD cross makes an ideal pet and is highly trainable.

OTHER CROSSES

There are innumerable crossbreeds in existence, and this book covers just a few. Breeders are always

The German Shepherd Lurcher is easy to train.

looking for ways to improve the Lurcher, so the emergence of new dogs is inevitable. The Lurcher's popularity as a pet dog has also meant that breeders are now concerned as much with temperament and appearance as they are with working ability. This has produced dogs with stunning good looks and biddable temperaments. From the point of view of the survival of the crossbreed, this can only be a good thing.

3 *Choosing A Lurcher*

Having decided that you want a Lurcher, you need to determine which type (see Chapter Two). Talk to other dog owners, read a few books, and contact dog clubs and trainers. You need to build up a profile of the mental and physical needs of each dog which appeals to you. Only after you have compared these profiles to the demands of your own lifestyle can you make a fair appraisal as to whether you can offer a dog a secure and happy life.

CHOOSING A PUPPY

There are some very good reasons for choosing a puppy as opposed to an adult dog. Probably the biggest advantage is the opportunity to provide correct socialisation. At a young age, a puppy can be introduced to other pets and people, and a wide variety of settings and experiences. Puppies soak up learning experiences more readily than older dogs, and training tends to be easier and quicker with a puppy, though not necessarily more sedate!

Puppies are not suitable for everyone, however. A puppy demands as much time as a newborn baby, and may actually require more. At least a human baby does not run around knocking things over, chew through electric cables, or mess on your new carpet! If you work full-time or live in a hectic household, a puppy might not be the right choice.

You can never be certain how a Lurcher puppy will turn out.

Another consideration is what the puppy will grow up to become. Genetic 'throwbacks' are still relatively common in Lurchers. The puppy which you thought would grow into a medium-sized smooth-coated Greyhound type could turn out to be a shaggy-haired giant – rare, but certainly possible!

FINDING A BREEDER

The option of purchasing a Lurcher puppy from a breeder is only really applicable to those who want a specific cross. Conscientious breeders can be found by contacting your local Lurcher club (as advertised in dog magazines or telephone directories). Breeders' own advertisements, or private-sale notices for home-bred litters, may appear in newspapers or on notice boards, but be sure to check the authenticity of such people and the concern which they demonstrate for the welfare of their dogs.

PUPPY FARMS

If you want to get your puppy from a breeder, take care that you are not caught out by the puppy farms (mills). These 'farms' operate on a scale of mass production, keeping puppies of numerous breeds in appalling conditions. Animals bought from such establishments have a high rate of genetic defects.

Puppy farms are normally obvious because of their size – usually much bigger than even the larger-scale reputable breeders. Another giveaway is the absence of the dam (the puppies' mother). If you ask to see the dam, and are given an excuse, do not buy a puppy. A genuine breeder will positively invite you to see the mother.

In the case of Lurchers, the managers of puppy farms have developed a new tactic. Instead of inviting people to view the dogs at the farm, these uncaring breeders take the dogs to country fairs and agricultural shows. If you are offered a dog in this way, you *must* refuse. Do not be coerced into looking either, since sympathy is a strong emotion and many dogs have been sold through the use of this tactic. If you see dogs being sold in this fashion, please inform the event organisers as soon as possible.

Pet shops sometimes offer Lurcher puppies for sale, but do not be tempted to buy this way. Often, pet shops act as outlets for

Take time to assess all members of the litter.

puppy farms, and there will be no specialist advice or support from an experienced breeder. Such dogs will have had little socialisation and are at a higher risk of infection.

VIEWING THE LITTER

To choose the right puppy you will need to see the whole litter with their mother. This will give you a much clearer impression of the character and temperament of each puppy. The way in which the puppies behave towards each other will demonstrate which individuals are boisterous, which are shy, which are noisy, and which are aggressive. The mother's behaviour towards the litter – whether she is affectionate or remote – is indicative of the puppy's future temperament.

When you view the litter, a good tip is to take along a squeaky toy. Stand a little way back, kneel down, make the toy squeal and see which puppies appear interested. The curious and confident puppy will first cock his head at you, and then follow the movement of the toy as you move it around. This shows that he has confidence and an interest in his surroundings. Pick him up carefully, while still kneeling. He should not struggle. Feel him all over, including the mouth and belly. The right puppy

A Lurcher puppy should be lively and inquisitive.

may protest a little but will not attempt to bite you or to put up a serious fight.

Do not be tempted to pick the runt, who is usually overly timid and prone to ill health. This is not to say that he will not make a good pet, only that he requires an experienced owner who is aware of all the pitfalls.

If the runt is a dubious choice, then the dominant puppy is even worse. Your chosen puppy must learn that your household is his new 'pack', and that he occupies the lowest position in it. The dominant puppy may challenge you constantly in a bid to increase his status in your home. If you have neither the authority nor the experience to put him in his place, your cute little puppy will be ruling the house in no time.

HEALTH CHECKS

There are a number of quick checks which you can make when you visit the litter. If your puppy fails any of them, think very carefully about purchasing him. There is nothing more devastating than buying a puppy only for him to die shortly afterwards.

- Carefully pick up the puppy. A healthy puppy should feel heavy and firm.
- The pup's ears should be clean and pink with no signs of a waxy discharge.
- The eyes should be clear and free of discharge.
- Check the teeth and gums. The milk teeth should be strong and white, while the gums should be pink and plump.
- The puppy's breath should not be too smelly. Some halitosis is to be expected – he is a dog – but too much indicates a problem.
- Check that the puppy's rear end is clean with no signs of discharge.
- Stroke the puppy, moving your hand both with the fur and against it. The hair should feel soft, neither too dry nor too

greasy. The puppy should not moult, and any skin which is displayed should be free of sores and minor irritations.

- Observe the pup's movement. There should be no signs of injuries.
- Look for lumps and bumps on the body.
- If you have *any* doubts, reconsider your decision. There will be other puppies and other litters in the future.

Once you have chosen your puppy, make an appointment with the vet for the next day.

OTHER CHECKS

Before purchasing your puppy, ask to see the vaccination certificates of the puppy's mother. Make a note of the inoculations she has received, and discuss them with your own vet. You need to be sure that the mother is fully protected and not in any danger of passing on any complaints to her litter.

CHOOSING AN ADULT DOG

For the would-be pet owner, an animal shelter is probably the best source of adult dogs. Rescue dogs are usually house-trained and well

socialised, and, once they have made the adjustment to their new home, they make wonderful companions. There is also the added benefit that the size and shape of the adult dog are immediately apparent.

Another advantage to taking on a rescue dog is that it causes far less disruption to your daily routine. For the pet owner who works, this is particularly important. A well-trained adult dog may normally be left alone for up to four hours. This time may be increased if there is more than one dog.

A good rescue centre will give you the opportunity to get to know a dog *before* you take him home, encouraging you to go for walks together. Rescue dogs will also have had a thorough check-up

Taking on an adult Lurcher is a rewarding experience.

A bitch may be more biddable and easier to train.

from the vet. This is especially important for Lurchers, who have often sustained injuries to their joints, legs and feet.

Your local newspaper, telephone directory, and the dog press will carry details of such establishments.

PAST HISTORY

The main problem with adopting an adult dog is that there may be underlying psychological problems, which only become apparent much later. Common symptoms of this are excessive guarding of food or people. Most of these problems can be treated or cured, but it takes a lot of time and patience. In extreme cases, it may be necessary to seek the help of a canine behaviourist.

As a pet owner, and especially if you are an inexperienced dog owner, it is unlikely that you will be faced with a 'problem dog'. Most rescue centres will not rehome a dog who has significant health or behavioural problems. Where such dogs are rehomed, the centre will make sure that the new owner is aware of the problems and the treatment necessary to overcome them.

HEALTH CHECKS

If you purchase or adopt an adult Lurcher, you will need to check for old (or current) injuries. Watch the dog as he moves around. Does he favour one leg when running, or limp slightly after a long walk? Some injuries can be cured by an experienced vet, but others may be permanent and result in arthritis as the dog ages.

You will also need to make sure that the dog has had all his vaccinations. A rescue centre will almost certainly have made sure of this, but you should still ask to see the evidence.

MALE OR FEMALE?

Choosing a dog or a bitch is largely a matter of personal choice, and there are advantages and disadvantages with both sexes.

BITCHES

Bitches tend to be a little more laid back than dogs and easier to train, although this is as much to do with good socialisation and individual character as it is with gender.

Taking on a bitch requires the owner to consider the option of spaying. For the pet owner, who has no intention of breeding from their crossbreed, spaying is highly recommended. It eliminates the risk of pyometra (a life-threatening womb infection) and substantially reduces the chances of your pet developing mammary tumours at a later age. Some owners argue that it leads to weight gain and incontinence, but there is little evidence to support either claim. A well-exercised, well-cared-for bitch should face none of these problems.

If you want to know more about spaying, consult your vet.

DOGS

Generally, dogs are considered to be more dominant and aggressive than bitches. However, a male who has been well trained should not display tendencies of either nature.

As with bitches, neutering is highly recommended for dogs belonging to the pet owner. If your dog has not been castrated, he may develop a habit of scent-marking,

not only in the garden but also in the home. Neutering is far more socially responsible and has important health benefits.

Castration may reduce aggressive and hypersexed behaviour if those behaviours are a product of too much testosterone (it will have no effect if bad handling is the cause). Castrated dogs are also at a much reduced risk of developing balinitis (inflammation of the glans penis) and prostate disorders. The procedure also prevents testicular cancer. As with spaying, consult your vet if you have any queries about castration.

Neutering is a sensible option for the male.

4 *Your New Puppy*

Before you bring your new puppy home, you will need to 'dog-proof' your home and garden, and make sure that you have all the necessary equipment.

PREPARING FOR PUP

The way to combine both an attractive open garden and a Lurcher is to erect an enclosure for your puppy in a quiet corner of the garden. This reduces the need for high-security fences around the remainder of the garden.

The den can be made using a wooden frame, filled in with wire mesh. This should result in a lightweight cage which can be easily moved out of the way when not in use. However, be sure not to make it too small. Lurchers need to be able to exercise sufficiently, and it is cruel to keep any animal in cramped conditions.

Make sure that your dog enclosure is not near any dangerous plants. These include ivy, laburnum, clematis and lilies. Also remember that many bulbs, such as daffodils, can be deadly if chewed and digested.

You will need to be especially aware of these plants if, for some reason, a dog enclosure is not a practical solution in your particular garden. If your Lurcher is to have the free run of your garden, all hazardous plants must be removed.

TOILET AREAS

It is a good idea to pick an area in the garden which you would like your dog to use as his regular toilet spot. While it is tempting to place the toilet area at the furthest point of the garden, remember that, when you toilet-train your puppy, you will need to make frequent dashes to the toilet area, so choose a spot which is out of sight but not too far from the back door.

Lurcher puppies can be great escape artists, so make sure your garden is securely fenced.

FENCING

Escape-proofing your entire garden can prove costly and time-consuming – especially if you want to do it in such a way that it does not detract from the pleasure of your garden. New fencing will need to be erected if the old is insufficient. 'Open' gates, such as those made of wrought iron, will need to be boarded up or meshed over. Wire mesh (e.g. chicken wire) will also need to be placed around any holes in the fencing, as well as around plants and potentially lethal features such as garden ponds. Make sure that the mesh fencing around the pond is the right height. Lurcher puppies grow very quickly and a barrier which is sufficient one week may be totally inadequate the next.

IDENTIFICATION

If, despite your best efforts, your dog manages to escape, there are certain steps which will maximise the likelihood of being reunited. You *must* make sure that your dog wears a collar with a name tag that bears your name and telephone number.

In addition, you can have a small microchip inserted underneath the skin between your dog's shoulder blades. The chip is the size of a grain of rice, and stores an electronic 'barcode'. When your dog is found, a scanner will be passed over his shoulder blades, and the 'barcode' will be revealed. When this is entered into a computer database, it discloses the details of the owner.

INDOOR PREPARATIONS

Get down on your hands and knees to achieve a 'puppy perspective'. Look for things that are within a puppy's reach, such as electrical wires or a dangling tablecloth. Remove any items of furniture which may become irreparably damaged, houseplants which may be poisonous, any items made of china or glass – basically anything that could be dangerous or expensive if chewed or eaten. You will need to do this in all the areas where your puppy will be allowed to roam.

MAKING A BED

There are all sorts of dog beds available, but there is no need to spend a lot of money on one. A cardboard box of the appropriate size will suffice, and can be thrown away and replaced as necessary. It is also completely safe. Avoid wicker baskets, which can be hazardous if chewed.

Line the bed with an old woolly jumper. Do not use a stuffed cushion – in no time at all your puppy will have torn a hole in it, and if he swallows the stuffing it could be very harmful to him.

A few days before you are due to collect your puppy, give the breeder one of your jumpers. Ask him to put it in with the puppies for a few days, and wrap the pup in it when you bring him home. This will give the pup something that smells familiar and will help him to settle in. When the jumper has been washed, wear it yourself for a couple of hours before replacing it in his bed.

CRATES AND PENS

A young dog cannot be watched all the time, so investing in a pen is a good idea. There are several options available. Many pet stores sell specialised dog crates. These are portable and collapse when not in use. Crates are ideal because they are multi-purpose, serving not only as an indoor cage, but also as a bed and a safe means of transporting your dog in the car.

Indoor-only alternatives to the crate include a second-hand baby playpen, and the wire-mesh hinged fireguards. Two of these fireguards can be fastened together, using plastic cable ties, to make a square-shaped enclosure. The beauty of this sort of pen is that it can be expanded as the puppy grows.

Whichever type of enclosure you choose, line the floor with an offcut of linoleum or vinyl floor-covering, and then cover it with newspaper. This will prevent the carpet from getting soaked when your puppy has an 'accident' or decides to sit in his water bowl.

Always make sure that your puppy has plenty of toys and distractions when he is in his pen. This way he will associate his cage with fun, rather than with boredom and isolation. Never leave him inside the pen for extended periods, however. Remember that he will need regular toileting, exercise and reassurance that you have not forgotten about him.

GATES

Stair- or baby-gates are another must. They will prevent your puppy from climbing the stairs before he is old enough to do so safely. Gates can also be used to restrict your puppy to certain areas of the house.

The removable types, which can be adjusted to fit any doorway or staircase, are the better option. Your puppy may be able to squeeze between the bars on some models, in which case you will need to weave a piece of cardboard through the bars.

FOOD BOWLS

Food bowls should be chosen with care. Stainless steel bowls are probably the best choice since they are chew-resistant, durable and dishwasher-safe. Plastic bowls will need replacing regularly – most dogs cannot resist the temptation of chewing them. Ceramic bowls should only be used if they are very strong and heavy. Make sure that the water bowl has a wide base, so that it cannot be tipped over.

ARRIVING HOME

The day you collect your new pet will be a very special one. Try to arrange an early collection time with the breeder. This means that you and your dog will have all day to get to know each other.

Most breeders will advise you to

The big moment comes when it is time to collect your puppy.

hold the pup during the journey home. This will help to make the experience less overwhelming for him, as well as providing him with some much-needed contact in place of his absent littermates. The pup is quite likely to urinate or vomit, so make sure you have plenty of newspaper to mop it up.

Your pup will not have been fed before collection, so, once you arrive home, you should give him a meal. This will help to reassure your puppy and will show him that you are his new 'pack'. After feeding, allow him to explore his new surroundings.

Once he has settled down a little, invite the neighbours round to meet the puppy. This gives you an opportunity to apologise in advance for any disturbances they may suffer as a result of the puppy, and it also begins the socialisation process. If your puppy is familiar with your neighbours then he is unlikely to bark every time they enter or exit the house or garden.

THE FIRST NIGHT

The first night that the puppy is without the comforting presence of his littermates can be difficult, but there are a number of preparations and guidelines to help the night run more smoothly.

When it is time to retire for the night, do so with a minimum of fuss. Make sure the puppy has relieved himself first, and then take him to his bed. Settle the pup in his warm comfortable bed, and soothe him to sleep. Once he is drowsy, slip away quietly. Leave a ticking clock or a quietly playing radio nearby. It will provide background noise and make your puppy feel that he is not alone.

If you are extremely lucky, the puppy will have a quiet night, but it is more likely that he will wake and begin to cry. It is very easy for me to advise you not to go back to the puppy when he cries during the night. Listening to a small animal keening and wailing can be heart-rending. Nevertheless, you must ignore his pleas. Failure to do so may result in a dog who grows into a nervous and clingy adult.

TOILET-TRAINING

Toilet-training is one of the more unsavoury aspects to raising a puppy. I prefer to use the 'direct method' as it trains your puppy to relieve himself in the same location as he will once he reaches maturity – so avoiding any difficult cross-over periods.

Your pup will usually need to go to the toilet straight after a meal, when he wakes up, and after periods of exercise or excitement. He will display certain behaviours, such as sniffing the floor and walking around in circles. This behaviour is your cue to pick up the puppy and take him outside to the spot which you want him to use.

While your puppy urinates or defecates, you need to repeat a chosen catchphrase for the action – 'Quickly now', or 'Do your business', for example.

There will, undoubtedly, be times when you are not quick enough to take your puppy outside, but he should soon realise the point of the exercise and stand by the door whining to go out. Over time, it should be possible to teach your dog to relieve himself on command, on a particular spot.

Once your Lurcher has been trained to relieve himself outside, it is a good idea to make a gravel bed in his toileting area. The bed can be kept clean by removing any faeces on a daily basis. Once a

Supervise your puppy closely in the first few weeks, and house-training should not pose a major problem.

week, the gravel bed should be sluiced with warm water which has had an animal-friendly detergent added. This should be followed by rinsing with clean, cold water, and then topping up the bed with fresh gravel. To maintain sanitary conditions, this procedure will need to be done once a week as standard, and more often during hot weather.

INOCULATIONS

As a puppy, your Lurcher should be vaccinated against distemper, hepatitis, leptospirosis, parvovirus and parainfluenza. Your vet may also recommend immunisation against kennel cough. When you take your puppy to the vet to discuss inoculations, ask about worming programmes and flea treatments. Always remember that your puppy will not be protected against the above diseases until two weeks after his last injection.

FEEDING

Like humans, all dogs are different. Each individual will have preferred foods and quantities. The breeder/rescue centre will have provided you with a diet sheet which you should follow. By keeping to the puppy's normal diet you will avoid causing him to have an upset stomach. The following is the type of advice which I give to

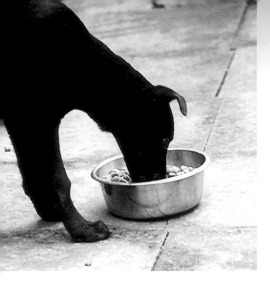

To begin with, stick to a diet that the puppy is used to.

owners of my puppies. If you experience any problems, contact your vet who will be happy to advise you on a suitable diet.

WEANING
Between the ages of six and twelve weeks, a puppy should be fully weaned. At this point he should be given four meals a day, routinely given at the same times each day.

- Meal one should be a meat meal – canned puppy food is ideal.
- Meal two should be milk-based. Do not use cows' milk, as many puppies are unable to digest this properly. Instead, use a specially prepared puppy milk or goats' milk. Mash up a cereal mix in these meals to give more substance.
- Meal three should be another meat-based meal.

- Meal four should be another milky meal.

THREE TO SIX MONTHS
At this age, the puppy should have three meals a day: two meat and one milk. Over time, replace the milk meal with another meat-based meal. Don't forget to make each of these three meals larger than when you were feeding four meals. You will need to compensate for the loss of the fourth meal at a time when your puppy is growing rapidly. Between the ages of three and six months, your puppy should be introduced to rawhide chews to strengthen his teeth and jaws.

SIX MONTHS ONWARDS
At the age of six months, you may cut your puppy's meals to two a day. Remember to enlarge the other meals accordingly. Start to introduce him to adult meals, perhaps mixing adult food with puppy food, or replacing one meal. Introduce the new food slowly, but aim to have your adolescent Lurcher on an adult diet by the end of the seventh month.

GROOMING
As an adult, your Lurcher will need regular grooming (see Chapter Five).

You can avoid all sorts of problems later on by familiarising your dog to grooming routines when he is a youngster.

COAT CARE

As soon as you bring your puppy home, you should habituate him to being brushed all over, using a brush suitable for his coat type (see Chapter Five). This includes his feet, tail, rear-end and face. Also, place him in the bath and run tepid water around his feet. This will get him used to the sound of the taps and the feel of the water.

TOOTH CARE

A regime for maintaining dental hygiene should begin while your puppy is very small. Your puppy should be used to having his muzzle touched and the inside of his mouth explored. He should raise no objections to your pulling aside his lips, gently prodding his gums, and inspecting his teeth. The best way to accustom your puppy to this is to brush his teeth once a week (see Chapter Five).

TEETHING

When your Lurcher pup is about four to six months old, he will begin teething. As with human infants, this can be very painful.

Make sure that your puppy has plenty to chew on to alleviate his symptoms.

Teething will pass in a short space of time, but keep a close eye on the new teeth and the puppy's gums to make sure that there are no problems developing. Regularly check that the deciduous teeth are not preventing the growth of the new teeth, or causing them to grow crookedly.

EXERCISE

Although the Lurcher is a running dog, you must be careful not to overdo your puppy's exercise. A little exercise, at frequent intervals, is the best regime to follow. Until the puppy reaches maturity, his joints are still forming, and too much exercise can damage their development. A half-mile circuit is plenty for a puppy.

Invest in an extendable lead, as no dog should be allowed to run free until he has had sufficient training and will return to his owner promptly when told. Begin by letting your puppy run around in the garden and then progressing to longer walks.

Remember that your puppy should have received all his inoculations before you take him beyond your home.

Playing in the garden will be sufficient exercise for the first few weeks.

SOCIALISATION

The socialisation process begins from the moment you collect your puppy, and will continue throughout the whole of your dog's life. Removing him from his mother and his littermates, and introducing him to your home, teaches the puppy to accept change and new experiences. A dog's character is mostly shaped during the first 16 weeks. Therefore, this is the ideal time in which to introduce your puppy to new people and experiences. It is an opportunity to help your puppy develop into a well-adjusted, responsive and confident dog.

As part of the socialisation process, your puppy should be taught some basic obedience exercises (see Chapter Six).

IN THE HOME

You may believe that your home is a safe haven, but, from a puppy's point of view, there are all sorts of alarming objects. Anything which makes a noise, such as the vacuum cleaner, has the potential to become frightening to your puppy. By leaving domestic appliances or other strange objects in full view all of the time, your puppy will become used to them.

It is then a short step to your puppy becoming accustomed to certain items making a noise or moving around.

OUT AND ABOUT

Take your puppy outside as often as possible. If he is waiting for his vaccinations, he can still be taken out as long as he is carried.

Show him everything which he is likely to encounter in his life, such as cars, buses, bicycles and motorbikes. Show him trees, birds, other dogs, other puppies, cats, dustbins and lamp-posts (obviously a favourite). Introduce him to people with funny haircuts or beards, people with hats on, and people wearing crash helmets, etc.

When your puppy is able to walk down the street in a calm manner, unperturbed by the various sights and sounds, take him further afield.

Accustom him to riding in a car (safely confined to a crate or strapped in a dog safety-harness), take him to your friends' houses, and take him to the bus station and the train station. Every experience counts.

CHILDREN

If you do not have children of your own, find a relative or friend who does. It is very important that your puppy learns to accept these small people who behave differently to adults.

While doing so, always supervise very closely – events can quickly get out of hand, even with a sweet-natured dog and well-behaved children.

If you carry your puppy, you will be able to take him out and about to socialise him before he has completed his inoculations.

5 *Adult Care*

If you have brought home an adult dog, you will need to make the same sort of preparations as for a puppy, i.e. make sure that the garden is securely fenced off, that all poisonous plants are removed, and that access to other plants and the garden pond is restricted. For an adult Lurcher, an eight-feet-high jump poses no challenges, so your fencing will need to take this into account.

FEEDING
In the wild, a dog will eat once every three to four days. The chances of successfully obtaining a meal are slim, so when a wild dog does have a meal he will gorge himself. Natural selection has responded to this pattern by altering the canine digestive system.

Domestic dogs share the same digestive system as their wild cousins, so it is very important to feed the correct quantity to your pet. If too much food is given, part of the meal will be retained in the dog's stomach for up to 24 hours. This is so that, in the event of a long period without a meal, the body can digest the left-over food and obtain the energy reserves from it. As a pet, it is unlikely that your Lurcher will go more than 24 hours without food, so, if too much food is given consistently, your dog will gain a lot of weight. Vets estimate that a third of all pet dogs are overweight due to being fed an incorrect diet in the wrong quantities. Watching your pet's body weight is especially important, as obesity is a potential killer for the Lurcher.

COMPLETE FOODS
Adult dogs are best fed on a high-quality complete dried food. Long-jawed dogs, such as the Lurcher, are prone to excessive plaque, and tartar build-up, and dried food helps to clean the teeth.

A complete diet suits most Lurchers.

If your Lurcher is used to canned or other 'moist' foods, you can make the switch by introducing a little of the dried food to your Lurcher's meat meal, and, over the next two weeks, reducing the amount of meat while increasing the quantity of dried food. Eventually, your dog should be eating the dried food alone.

If your dog appears unhappy about changing to complete food, soak part of the food in warm water. This makes it more palatable. Mix some of the dampened food in with the drier, more crunchy food. Over time, increase the dry food and reduce the moistened.

OTHER FOODS

If your Lurcher likes to chew on bones, make sure that you give him roast-beef bones, which are available from pet stores. Never give your dog any other form of bone. Some types can splinter and cause fatal internal injuries. Always supervise your dog when he is gnawing on a bone.

Treats are fine for Lurchers, as long as they are specialist canine treats. Do not give chocolate intended for human use, as this is highly toxic. In the interests of controlling weight, remember to reduce the size of your dog's meal if he has had a large number of treats that day.

FEEDING PRACTICES

Most dogs eat from a bowl which is placed on the floor. Running dogs have long legs and necks, and sometimes find it difficult to eat from floor-level bowls. In effect, their body is so contorted that they have to swallow upwards, against gravity. Therefore, for the adult Lurcher, it is a good idea to purchase a bowl stand. A stand raises the dog bowl from the floor by as much as 12 inches (30 centimetres), making eating a much simpler activity for your dog. The stands are available from most pet stores, and are made of metal, so, once purchased, a single stand should last a lifetime.

Try not to feed your dog less than an hour before or after exercise. This will help to prevent a condition called Gastric Torsion, more commonly known as Bloat (see Chapter Eight). Another tip is to make sure that you feed your Lurcher *after* you and your family have eaten. This serves as a reminder to your pet that he ranks at the bottom of the family hierarchy.

It is important to remember that the feeding information contained here is a rough guide only.

A bowl stand enables the Lurcher to eat more easily.

Whichever food you choose to give to your pet, make sure you follow the manufacturer's guidelines. If you have any queries or problems, always consult your vet.

GROOMING

Generally, Lurchers are among the easiest of dogs to care for when it comes to grooming. They are naturally clean. Every dog owner develops a grooming routine which works for them. The following practices are those which I have used very successfully with my own dogs. If they do not prove to be suitable for you, adapt them, seek further advice from another expert, or try a grooming parlour.

Grooming sessions are about more than simply making your Lurcher look clean and attractive. They are an important means of checking your Lurcher's health. Each session should be preceded by your running your hands all over the dog's body to check for lumps or other problems. This should include checking for wounds which do not appear to be healing properly.

COAT CARE

Lurchers usually have either a rough coat or a smooth coat. Each

The smooth-coated Lurcher is easy to care for.

needs to be treated differently. Smooth-coated dogs need to be brushed every two to three days with a bristle brush or hound glove. A shine can be given to the coat by using a chamois leather or velvet cloth, which can be wrapped around the hand and stroked firmly over the dog's body after brushing. Rubber grooming brushes, or mitts, are especially useful when your dog comes into moult.

Lurchers with rough coats, such as Deerhound crosses, will need brushing every day with a soft, slicker-type brush to remove dead hair. Tangles should be teased out with a comb. It is worth noting

that rough-coated dogs can have a fine downy undercoat which is waterproof, though the coarser topcoat may not be. After muddy walks, or playing in the rain, you will need to towel-dry your dog. Some people like to finish with a hairdryer, on its lowest setting, as this makes the coat less likely to tangle and easier to brush. Be warned though – not all dogs will tolerate this and some may be badly frightened by the experience.

BATHING

Lurchers need bathing only once or twice per year. Most owners prefer to bathe their dogs in the spring and late summer – when the dogs moult – as this helps to remove loose hair.

Some dogs will quite happily endure bath times, while others will hate it. If you acquired your Lurcher as a puppy then effective socialisation should mean that you do not experience any difficulties. However, if you bought an adult or a rescue dog, then the procedure might not go so smoothly. Make bathing as enjoyable as possible, involving lots of toys and treats. Before too long your dog should associate bathing with fun.

When you bathe your dog, always put a rubber mat in the

bottom of the bath to stop your dog slipping. Use a quality shampoo which has been specially designed for dogs. Coal-tar types are particularly good. Conditioners are also available if you wish to pamper your Lurcher, but they are not strictly necessary. Whichever products you use, always follow the instructions and be sure to use the correct quantities.

The most important point when bathing a dog is to rinse away the shampoo or conditioner. Most products have a habit of clinging to the thick coat of the dog, and can take a considerable amount of time and water to remove. Failure

The rough-coated Lurcher, like this Irish Wolfhound cross, needs daily attention.

to remove all the detergent can result in skin complaints and dull-looking hair.

After bathing, a brisk rub with a towel is all that is necessary in good weather. In cooler conditions, a thorough towel-dry followed by an hour in front of the radiator does the trick. If preferred, you can use a hairdryer, on its coolest setting, as described above.

EYES

Every time you groom his coat, you should check your dog's eyes and clean them, if necessary. Examine each eye carefully for abnormalities, such as severely bloodshot whites and lumps on the eyelids. The eyes should be cleaned by gentle wiping with cotton wool (cotton) soaked in cooled boiled water to sterilise. Pay special attention to the corners and wipe away any discharge and muck which may have accumulated.

EARS

Check the ears for excessive wax, discharge or signs of mites. Clean them with moist cotton wool. Never be tempted to progress beyond the outer ear as inserting objects into the ear canal can cause pain, injury, or even deafness. If there are any foreign bodies in the ear canal, or if there is a severe build-up of dirt or wax, consult your vet. He or she will be happy to clean the ears professionally, or will recommend a specialist ear-cleaning product for you to use. If you use such products, always follow the manufacturer's guidelines very carefully.

TOOTH CARE

Lurchers are prone to plaque and the build-up of tartar. Both of these complaints can lead to gum inflammation or disease, ulceration of the mouth, and complete loss of teeth. Bearing in mind that prevention is the best cure, it is vital to brush your dog's teeth regularly. Once a week is a good habit to develop.

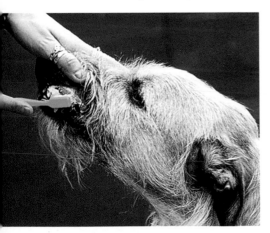

Teeth should be cleaned regularly.

Canine toothbrushes can be purchased from your vet, who will be happy to offer advice and tips. He or she will demonstrate the procedure if you have doubts about doing it for the first time. Never use a human toothbrush, as these can damage the inside of the dog's mouth. The same warning applies to toothpaste – only use a canine 'enzymatic' paste. Again, these are available from your vet, and come in all kinds of delicious flavours such as liver or chicken.

Most dog owners find it easiest to work from the front teeth to the back. If you own a dog who is intimidated by the experience, or who protests, you will need an assistant to hold the dog. Never let your pet's distress dissuade you from regular dental care, however, since it will only cause him more distress in the long term. If you feel unable to persist, make regular appointments with your vet or local dog groomer.

When you brush your dog's teeth, keep an eye out for any signs of swelling or inflammation of the gums, damage to the tongue, or chipped, broken, or missing teeth. A little bleeding after brushing is quite normal, but if it persists or is heavy, take your dog to your vet immediately.

FOOT CARE

You should check your dog's paws after every walk, to make sure that there are no signs of damage. Pay particular attention to the pads and between the toes.

Occasionally, you will need to trim your Lurcher's claws and dewclaws. The frequency of this varies from animal to animal. Some younger, well-exercised animals never require it. The easiest way to keep claws short is to include 15 minutes of 'road work' every other day. This means walking your dog along a path or on concrete – it has the benefit of wearing down your dog's claws naturally. You can trim your Lurcher's claws at home if necessary, but ask your vet to show you how to do this properly.

EXERCISE

There is a popular misconception that running dogs require vast amounts of exercise. Every dog should have regular and sufficient exercise the Lurcher needs no more than any other similarly sized dog. A Lurcher should be walked two to three times a day, and anything between a five-mile hike and thirty minutes' frenetic activity in a small football-pitch-sized field is adequate.

The Lurcher needs no more exercise than any other breed of dog.

6 *Training And Troubleshooting*

For the majority of Lurchers it would appear that instinct far outweighs intelligence. This will present problems before, during and after training sessions. Therefore, it is important to enrol at a top-quality training school, where the trainers will know how to work with this conflict and help you to train your dog to be a well-behaved and responsive animal.

For owners of 'difficult' dogs, the latter half of this chapter should help you to pinpoint and rectify certain problems, although in some cases it may be necessary to seek help from a professional canine behaviourist (your vet will be able to refer you).

TRAINING CLASSES

The best way to find a good training club is by word of mouth. Alternatively, look for adverts in your local pet stores and vet's surgery, and ask your vet and other dog owners for recommendations.

It is well worth making a visit to various training schools *before* you enrol your dog. Make a note of how many people (and dogs) attend the class, whether the dogs and owners appear happy, and whether the trainer is competent and in control. The classes should be structured into different levels, including a beginners' puppy-training class, and classes for the more advanced.

Examine the trainer's methods. If choke chains are used, do not enrol. Choose a trainer who uses a reward-based method, since dogs learn through repetition and reward.

Many countries have a trade association of dog trainers, where membership is open only to those who demonstrate effective and humane techniques. Contact your national kennel club to obtain a list of association members in your area.

GENERAL TRAINING

Training should begin from the moment you bring your Lurcher home. If, at this point, he is a puppy, you will obviously have to wait until he has had all his injections before enrolling him at a training school. However, this does not mean that you cannot begin basic training at home.

The exercises described below are suitable for a young puppy and for an older dog, although the latter will hopefully have undergone some training previously.

Always remember that, just as a competent trainer will not use punishment when training a dog, neither should you. Scolding or physical abuse only leads to resentment and fear. Instead, use other distractions to divert his attention, and praise lavishly whenever your Lurcher gets something right. Where treats are required, give your Lurcher cat

A training club will give your Lurcher the opportunity to mix with other dogs.

biscuits. They are quite small, will not fill him up and are seen as more exciting because they are different from his normal food.

COMMANDS

The most important rule is to be consistent with your commands. Your puppy will never understand what is required of him if you change commands or combine them. For example, "Sit" means sit and "Down" means down. If you ask your dog to "Sit Down" you are giving him two separate commands and will confuse him. Keep your commands short and simple.

A treat held above the head will encourage your puppy to Sit.

SIT

With your pet in a standing position, hold a treat on the end of his nose. Slowly lift the treat upwards and backwards. The dog's rear should hit the floor. As it does so, say "Sit"', praise him and then give him the biscuit. Always use a release command before letting your pet move from the sitting position. "Finish" is the normal one and can be used to end any command. Repeat the exercise, on different occasions, until your pet will respond straight away.

Once he reaches this stage, slowly cut down the treats. Instead of giving your Lurcher a treat every time he responds successfully, make it every other time, then every third time, etc. Do not make the mistake of pushing down on your dog's bottom when you teach this command. If you do this, the dog learns to respond to your touching his rear, not to the word "Sit".

DOWN

Kneel down to the dog's level and hold the treat on the end of his nose. Proceed as if you were teaching the Sit command, but *do not* tell him to "Sit". Instead, with the treat still on the dog's nose, bring it slowly down and forwards while encouraging the dog to follow. If he lies down, say "Down", praise him, and give him the treat. Do not forget to say "Finish" before you let him get up.

A good tip when teaching your dog to lie down is to use a piece of furniture. For example, place your pet into a sitting position facing a chair. Place yourself on the other side and place your arm through the gap between the chairlegs. Bring your hand – containing a treat – slowly down under the chair. The treat should end up on the floor directly underneath the chair. The chair restricts the dog, so that he cannot stand up and move forwards to the treat but is forced to lie down to reach it.

STAY

You should begin to teach your dog to Stay at mealtimes. When he comes for his food, ask him to "Sit". Now tell him to "Stay" and wait for a few seconds before you give him his meal. Gradually increase the length of time your Lurcher has to wait for his meal.

Once your dog has mastered the Stay waiting for his food, teach him to Stay where and whenever you demand.

RECALL

The Recall is a vital command to learn, but one of the most difficult to teach. A good time to start is at dinner. Let your dog out into the garden and close the door. Prepare his meal, open the door and shout the dog's name followed by "Come". If your pet knows it is dinner time, he will come rushing into the kitchen with very little encouragement. Immediately after he arrives, take a light hold of his collar and praise him lavishly, then give him his dinner. Do this every time you feed him.

The next stage is to call your dog to you when you are both in the garden. Let him play, call his name followed by "Come", and encourage him to you. When he comes to you, lightly hold his collar *and only then* give him a treat and praise. Repeat until your Lurcher is performing this action reliably.

Progressing to the stage where your dog can be let off-lead in public, knowing that he will come when you call, is best left to training classes. However, the above exercise will have cemented the foundation for future training in your Lurcher's mind.

LEAD-TRAINING

While your dog is on the lead, you should be in charge. It should be the owner who sets the direction and pace, and the dog should follow quite happily. Only when the dog is let off the lead should he be allowed to frolic to his heart's content, and even then he should return as soon as he is called (see below).

Those who have taken on an adult dog are best advised to attend a training class, because overcoming bad habits is far harder than starting from scratch. For owners of puppies, the first step is to introduce your new pet to a lead. Clip a lead to your pup's collar and then let him play and wander about with it still attached. Always supervising your puppy, repeat the exercise for ten minutes throughout the day until he is comfortable with the lead.

Once your puppy has come to accept the lead, pick up the end and walk in a straight line, encouraging the puppy to follow you. Use treats or toys if they are necessary, and reward your dog for 'nice' walking. If your pet starts to pull, you should stop and encourage him back to you. When the lead is slack again, and you

Give lots of praise and encouragement when you are lead-training.

have the dog's attention once more, continue the exercise. A good tip is to walk slightly faster than the puppy's normal walking pace so that he has to work to keep up with you.

Only practise lead-training for a few minutes at a time – a puppy's attention span is very short. Little and often is always the rule when trying to teach any lesson to a puppy. When he can walk with you in a straight line, introduce a few turns, using treats or toys to encourage your puppy to stay at heel.

BEHAVIOURAL PROBLEMS

Some Lurchers can be hyperactive, while others are prone to laziness.

Overexuberance is at the root of many behavioural problems, such as chasing and jumping up. Both of these problems can be overcome with good training and socialisation.

The more severe problems associated with Lurchers are stealing and guarding. Unfortunately, these are not quite so easy to eradicate as chasing or jumping up.

CHASING

Chasing is relatively easy to overcome. Your dog cannot help his desire to chase after small furry objects – it is what he has been bred for. However, you can override his natural instinct with the Leave command.

"LEAVE"

This command should be spoken loudly enough for the dog to take

Many behavioural problems are the result of over-exuberance.

notice, but without being a shout, and should be in the sternest voice you can muster.

Take two treats and place one in each hand. Kneel down at the same level as the dog, and extend your arm with your hand open and the treat held in the palm. Offer the biscuit to the dog, then, as he comes forward to take it, quickly close your hand around the treat and say "Leave". Your Lurcher will probably take a step back in shock, and look very confused. Keeping that hand closed, open your other hand to reveal the second treat. Say "Take it". Your Lurcher should come forward, warily, to take the reward. When he does so, praise him lavishly.

Repeat the exercise until your dog refrains from taking the treat except on command. Then, you can progress to other objects which you would prefer to be left alone, such as shoes.

JUMPING UP

While your Lurcher is a puppy, jumping up may not appear to be much of a problem. As an adult, however, it is dangerous. The solution is to discourage it from the start. When your Lurcher tries to jump up, ignore his behaviour,

Jumping up can cause problems in an adult Lurcher.

turn your back, refuse to make eye contact, and do not speak to him – do not acknowledge his presence in any way. When the dog gives up and has all four paws on the ground, kneel down to his level and pet and talk to him. The dog will quickly learn that jumping up is ignored whereas waiting patiently until you descend to his level elicits a much nicer response. Please note that this will only work if every person who meets your dog does the same. Explain to the rest of the family, your friends and regular guests what you want them to do and why. People are normally quite understanding.

STEALING

Almost every Lurcher possesses this unfortunate habit to a greater or lesser extent. Even when the Lurcher concerned is otherwise well behaved and aware that he will be severely chastised for stealing, he seems unable to help himself. The main problem is that they are amazingly good at it, and rarely get caught in the act.

The average Lurcher will steal anything – from rubber gloves to plastic flowerpots. Food is always preferred, but your Lurcher will attempt to steal any item left out, and, once he has it in his possession, you will have great difficulty trying to retrieve it.

If you are around to see your Lurcher stealing, a firm "Leave" should stop him. However, it will not prevent him from making the attempt in your absence. Therefore, you will need to take preventative measures. Do not leave dangerous objects, such as knives or bottles of tablets lying around, and generally try to put things in cupboards or drawers. You will very quickly learn to become incredibly tidy if you own a Lurcher!

GUARDING

Most dogs possess the guarding instinct, and it is normally associated with food. However, for some Lurchers, the problem can develop from guarding food to guarding toys, a favourite bed or chair, and even an owner. If this behaviour is not controlled, your dog will display similar behaviour when he feels anything of 'his' is under threat, and he may develop a tendency to start fights.

The solution is to consult your trainer or vet at the first signs of possessiveness. Hopefully, they will be able to advise you how to control the problem. In severe cases, it may be necessary to consult an animal behaviourist, or to consider castration if testosterone is the root cause. Be aware, however, that possessive behaviour is often indicative of a hierarchy problem, and the dog should be firmly reminded of his position at the bottom of the family pack.

OTHER PROBLEMS

If you have any doubts or

A well-socialised Lurcher will learn not to be over-possessive.

problems whatsoever, seek the advice of a professional. Leaving behavioural problems, and hoping they will resolve of their own accord, is very foolish. In most cases the problem gets worse. Very often, talking to others about your Lurcher's idiosyncrasies will reveal that other dogs have suffered similar problems. There is a wealth of experience and advice out there on which you can call, and no one will think any the worse of you for asking for help.

7 The Active Lurcher

The Lurcher is a naturally versatile animal, and has a rapidly growing following. There are hundreds of Lurcher clubs all over the country, and each offers the Lurcher owner plenty of opportunity to participate in a wide range of activities with their dog.

DOG SHOWS

The Lurcher is not a pedigree breed. It does not, therefore, have an official Breed Standard (a 'blueprint' describing the dog's appearance and characteristics) to which each Lurcher must conform. Unfortunately, this means that, no matter how beautiful your dog, you will not be able to exhibit him in a national kennel club dog show. Championship shows such as Crufts or Westminster are never going to be anything more than a dream.

However, the various Lurcher clubs frequently host their own dog shows, and there are also many local dog shows which you can attend. Your breed club will have details of all forthcoming events.

LURCHER SHOWS

This type of show is aimed at the Lurcher enthusiast, and will be attended by many breeders and many working-dog owners, but there are plenty of other activities which the pet owner can enjoy, such as racing.

Being a running dog, racing is, to some extent, in the blood of every Lurcher. The racing events at a Lurcher show are a highlight – for the dogs and the spectators. Races are usually over a minimum distance of 200 yards (180 metres), although this can vary from venue to venue.

The dogs chase a lure, which is normally a scented cloth attached to a mechanical winch, usually mounted on the front or back of a vehicle. Each dog is given a colour (a handkerchief, for example), which is attached to the dog's collar. This helps to identify him as he runs along the track. At the end of the track, a false lure is thrown in. The dogs, distracted by the false lure, stop running, and the race ceases.

If you want to enter your dog in a race, do not be put off by lack of experience. People will be only too happy to guide you through the racing process, and your dog will take to it as if he has been doing it all his life.

If you decide to participate, you will need a muzzle. Introduce your dog to wearing a muzzle from as early an age as you can, just for

Showing is an increasingly popular hobby among Lurcher owners.

short periods at a time. Most get used to them very quickly. Always choose a plastic, Greyhound-type muzzle. The wire muzzles can be dangerous.

You will also need a dog who will return to you on command, since there is nothing more annoying than an out-of-control dog at a show. If you would like to attend a Lurcher show, contact a local Lurcher club or breeder. Alternatively, keep an eye out for advertisements in newspapers, local shops and clubs. Most Lurcher shows take place at country fairs, which are well advertised.

FUN SHOWS

Fun shows are much more of a family day out and are usually very enjoyable. The show is normally divided into several classes, such as Best dog under a certain height, Best-kept coat, Most appealing eyes, etc.

To enter a class, you will need to arrive early on the day of the show and register. A point to note is that you will not be allowed to enter if you cannot produce a valid vaccination certificate for your dog, issued from your vet at the time of your dog's booster.

Although the winners will take great pride in their achievement,

If you work hard at training your Lurcher in basic obedience, you may graduate to Competitive Obedience.

the emphasis is very definitely on fun, not competitiveness, so do not feel too intimidated to take part. A show schedule will guide you through the entry process.

OBEDIENCE COMPETITIONS

If your Lurcher has responded very well to basic obedience training, then you may like to try advancing to Competitive Obedience.

This is a much more formal style of obedience. Commands such as "Sit", "Down" and "Come" are all used, but the dog has to respond immediately and in a very precise and standardised way.

There are also more complicated routines such as heelwork, where the dog has to walk by your side with and without a lead.

Top-level Obedience is difficult and competitive, although there

If you can establish a good level of control, your Lurcher will do well in Agility.

are classes for beginners. Given that Obedience is an extension of basic training, your dog's puppy trainer will be happy to advise you on how to take up the sport if you are interested.

One word of warning – Lurchers are not renowned for their Obedience ability, and training them takes time. One of my current dogs has taken more than two years to reach competition standard (although he has done quite well at fun shows).

Probably the better alternative for pet owners is Lurcher Obedience. Lurcher clubs often host Obedience events at their shows, which are open to anybody with a dog that has been trained to normal pet standards. These competitions are great fun, and are suitable for the budding Obedience competitor as well as those who just want to have a go.

AGILITY

Agility is basically an obstacle course for dogs. The dog has to negotiate features, such as tunnels and jumps, in a certain order and as fast as he can. The winner is the dog who makes the fewest mistakes and completes the course in the fastest time.

The obstacles include a variety of different jumps, the heights of which depend on the size of the dog.

In the UK, most Lurchers are included in the Standard Class (17 inches/43 centimetres high or over), in which the jumps are 30 inches (76 cms) high.

In the US, the majority of dogs will face jumps of 20 inches (51 cms) in height.

The other obstacles include:

- **Tyre jump**
  The dog has to jump through the hole in the middle of a specially-prepared tyre.

- **Long jump**
  A series of planks are fitted together to make a long jump. The dog must clear the length of the planks when he jumps.

- **Tunnels**
  These can be hoop tunnels (where the dog can see out of the other side) and/or collapsible tunnels (where the dog has to push his way through).

- **Weave poles**
  The dog has to weave his way through a line of poles.

Bred for speed and agility, the Lurcher takes the hurdles in his stride.

- **See-saw**
  This is like a child's see-saw. The dog has to walk along its entire length negotiating the change in balance.

- **Elevated dog walk**
  This is similar to a gymnast's beam, and the dog has to walk along it.

- **'A' frame**
  This is a tall, A-shaped obstacle, which the dog has to scale.

- **Pause table**
  The dog must jump on to the pause table and remain in a Sit or Down for a specified period of time (which is usually no more than a few seconds).

If Agility appeals to you, contact your national kennel club, who will inform you of your nearest club – there is bound to be one relatively close to you as the sport is so popular. The club will teach you and your Lurcher how to tackle the obstacles safely and successfully.

Please do not attempt to teach your pet Agility without a

All Lurchers thrive on being given something to do.

qualified instructor, as this is highly dangerous for you and your dog.

A registered Agility club will also encourage you to enter competitions once you and your dog have reached the appropriate standard. Lurchers seem to have a natural flair for this activity, and it is great fun at whatever level you wish to enter.

WORKING DOGS

Lurchers have a working heritage, and many of these dogs are still employed as working animals. Even pet dogs, when trained to work, seem to adapt very quickly and derive great enjoyment from it.

In the past, Lurchers were bred mainly to hunt rabbits and hares, and to control fox populations on agricultural land and game shoots.

Today's working Lurchers are often found working in this capacity and play a very valuable role in maintaining the stability of the countryside.

There are numerous books available on the subject of working dogs, which you can read to find out whether the working tradition is appropriate for your dog.

Your Lurcher club will also be able to advise you on how to start your dog working, as well as offering trial experiences.

AND FINALLY...

As a final word, I would urge all Lurcher owners to try at least one of these activities. A Lurcher who is not stimulated in mind and body has a tendency to become lazy and indifferent to the world around him. Taking an interest in any, if not all, of these activities will save your pet from becoming a couch potato. These activities also offer you, the Lurcher owner, an opportunity to broaden your horizons and meet new people – all of whom will share your love of these truly amazing animals.

8 *Health Care*

Crossbreeds tend to be more hardy than pure-bred dogs, and the Lurcher is no exception. The most common complaint suffered by Lurchers is the constant presence of minor cuts and scratches on their legs, normally due to negotiating bramble patches and stony ground at high speed.

Taking good care of your Lurcher will prevent many illnesses from ever developing, but it is important to remember that all dogs can become ill unexpectedly. For this reason, it is important to register your dog with a reliable and competent vet.

Your Lurcher should visit the vet twice a year as standard, and more often if regular treatment is required. If, at any time, you are concerned about the health of your pet, do not hesitate to take him to the vet immediately.

CHOOSING A VET

You should choose and register with a vet before you even arrange to collect your Lurcher. As with breeders, boarding kennels and training classes, the best method of choosing a vet is through personal recommendation, and remember that the closest vet may not necessarily be the best.

When you take your new dog to the vet's surgery for the first time, remember to take along any vaccination certificates which your dog may have. Your vet will give your Lurcher a thorough examination, and discuss inoculations, worming treatments and flea control with you. This is the time to ask any questions you may have concerning feeding, exercise and grooming.

VACCINATIONS

In my opinion, vaccinations are essential and should be

compulsory. Without the correct inoculations, a dog is unprotected against four of the most lethal diseases, and he also poses a risk to other animals.

If you own a puppy, and the dam was vaccinated, then your puppy will be protected up to the age of eight to ten weeks. This is because the mother's milk acts as a temporary vaccine.

Puppies are usually given their first 'jabs' at ten weeks, with the booster following two weeks later. Only after this second injection can the dog be safely taken out of the home to exercise and to meet other dogs.

Adult dogs with no history of vaccinations, such as those obtained from rescue centres, will have already seen a vet while under the care of the shelter staff. As soon as you have chosen your dog, the centre staff should inform you fully of the dog's medical history. In turn, you should make sure that this information is passed on to your new vet.

PARVOVIRUS

Parvovirus is a relatively new disease. The first outbreaks occurred in the 1970s, in America, Australia, and Europe. The virus attacks the heart,

quickly causing death.

Symptoms begin with severe vomiting, diarrhoea and dehydration, and death normally follows within 24 hours.

DISTEMPER

Canine distemper is still common in areas where there are high numbers of unvaccinated strays. It is a viral infection which is carried on the nose or pads of the feet and makes them appear thick and leathery – hence the 'hardpad' name which is given to one of the variants of the disease.

There are three stages of infection, making the illness very protracted. The first stage is known as the digestive stage. At this point the dog suffers from vomiting, diarrhoea and loss of appetite, in conjunction with a high temperature and fever.

The second stage affects the respiratory system. The same symptoms as the first stage are present, but with the addition of laboured breathing and attacks of coughing.

The final stage attacks the nervous system. The dog is racked with muscle cramps, spasms and, often, paralysis. This eventually results in the death of the dog. There is no effective cure for

distemper, so it is vital to ensure that your dog is protected by the preventative vaccination.

LEPTOSPIROSIS

Leptospirosis is caused by bacteria which live in the urine of infected animals, usually rats. Dogs contract the disease by eating urine-affected material or walking through puddles of infected urine. If the dog has cuts in his mouth or on his pads, the bacteria present in the urine manages to enter the bloodstream, causing infection.

There are two types of infection. The first causes irreparable damage to the kidneys. In severe cases, these organs may fail completely and cause death.

The symptoms of this illness include vomiting and an extremely high temperature. The second, rarer, type of leptospirosis, causes jaundice and liver damage and can be passed on to humans.

The symptoms include pain in the stomach and lower back, and yellow eyes. Again, the best form of treatment is prevention by vaccination, although it can be cured quite quickly if caught early enough.

HEPATITIS
Today, infectious canine hepatitis (Rubarth's disease) is rare.

Occasionally, singular infections occur in male dogs up to a year old.

The symptoms include intense thirst, fever and attacks of cramp, with the dog becoming very weak. A peculiarity of this disease is that the cornea of the eye turns blue, giving rise to the common name 'blue eye'.

Normally, dogs that survive the first forty-eight hours will make a full recovery.

PARASITE CONTROL
Most dogs will be affected by parasites during their lifetime. There are two classifications for parasites, and these are external and internal.

EXTERNAL PARASITES

The most common types of external parasites are fleas and lice. Occasionally a dog may contract ticks.

FLEAS

Apart from the incessant scratching by the pet, fleas can be identified by back-combing your pet's fur and looking for flea dirt. This will look like black dandruff. Closer inspection of the coat, close to the skin, should reveal the fleas themselves. Fleas are black or brown in colour and move rapidly through the fur.

Upon discovery, bedding and all other surfaces, including carpets and furniture, should be thoroughly cleaned, using a specialist anti-flea product.

All soft furnishings are likely to contain the eggs of your dog's fleas. These can remain dormant for up to a year before hatching, so, even if you treat your dog, you may not have successfully eradicated the problem.

Treatment for fleas has improved dramatically over the last few years, and your vet will be happy to advise you on the appropriate treatment for your Lurcher.

Do not forget that, if one pet in the house is found to have fleas, then all other pets need to be treated as well.

LICE

Canine lice are much the same as human lice. Adult lice and their eggs (which are glued to the fur) are normally found around the head and ears of your pet. In extreme cases, lice can actually be seen walking on the skin of your dog.

Unlike fleas, lice will only affect dogs and are not transferable to other pets. A fine-toothed comb run gently through the fur will trap the eggs and lice and remove them.

The best treatment for these parasites is a high-quality insecticidal shampoo, which can be purchased from your vet.

TICKS

Ticks usually originate from sheep or hedgehogs, and are picked up by your dog when out for a walk. The ticks jump on the dog and bury their mouths into the skin, feeding on the dog's blood. They look like white peas when engorged, and removal, unless you are experienced, is best left to your vet.

INTERNAL PARASITES

Two of the most common internal parasites to affect dogs are round-worms and tapeworms. Both are easily preventable with orally-administered treatments which can be provided by your vet.

ROUNDWORMS

Roundworms (*Toxocara canis*) are present in nearly every puppy. The puppy is infected by the mother while still in the womb, or by ingesting her contaminated milk.

By the time the puppy is two weeks old, the worms will be fully grown and living in the intestines. However, as the dog matures, he becomes immune to the worms and usually passes them naturally at around six months old.

Puppies who are severely infected will be slow-growing, weak, suffering from diarrhoea, with a pot-bellied appearance. Other symptoms include the presence of eggs in the dog's faeces.

In recent years there has been a lot of publicity about Toxocara causing blindness and brain damage in children who have contracted it through contact with canine faeces. The disease is extremely rare, but it is serious.

Reputable breeders should start worming their litters from the age

of two weeks, and this should continue once a month until the dog is six months old. After this, your dog should be treated regularly for the rest of his life.

TAPEWORMS

Tapeworm eggs are carried by fleas and lice. When a dog grooms himself, licking and nibbling the coat and skin, he may ingest one of these parasites. If this happens, the dog becomes a host.

An infected dog will appear to have grains of rice in his faeces or in the hair around his rear. These are probably eggs. If your pet loses his appetite, and his coat feels dry and spiky, you should take him to the vet for a proper examination. Stool samples containing the offending eggs should also be taken to the vet. Always remember that prevention is better than cure.

HEARTWORM

Heartworm disease, caused by a type of roundworm, is found mainly in tropical and subtropical regions. In temperate climates, only imported animals suffer from the disease. The parasite is carried by mosquitoes, and, once transmitted to the dog, develops into long, thin worms up to 11.5 inches (30 cms) in length.

The worms, which live in the right ventricle of the heart, cause the dog to suffer from breathlessness after exercise. Other symptoms include coughing and a thin, unkempt appearance. The disease is fatal if left untreated.

COMMON AILMENTS

Although they are generally among the healthier types of dogs, there are certain ailments which characteristically affect Lurchers.

MUSCLE INJURIES

Lurchers have evolved to be sophisticated running machines.

Like any highly trained human athlete, a Lurcher is susceptible to injuries which affect muscles and joints.

The most common muscle injuries occur in the shoulders. This is a result of the dog's weight distribution, which places up to 60 per cent of the weight on the forelegs when running. The massive muscles in the hindlegs are used almost exclusively for pushing the animal forward, which, while useful for acceleration, is not particularly effective for stopping. When a Lurcher tries to slow down or stop, he braces his forelegs and tries to back-pedal with his hindlegs. The stress which this places on the shoulders can cause injury.

Signs that your Lurcher is suffering from a muscle injury are limping and stiffness, especially after exercise. The affected muscle may feel hot to the touch and, in most cases, the dog will show signs of pain, especially when you try to touch the affected area.

Make the dog as comfortable as possible and take him to the vet. An animal who is limping on forelegs or hindlegs, but does not appear to be in any major discomfort, may have damaged

STOMACH UPSETS

Lurchers are prone to stomach disorders due to the reduced size of the digestive organs, which must occupy a smaller lower-body cavity.

Most stomach upsets are uncomfortable rather than life-threatening, but they are unpleasant for dog and owner alike.

The usual symptoms are loose bowel movements. Most stomach upsets are probably caused by the Lurcher's habit of eating any foul-smelling material – in fact, it seems that the more disgusting it is, the greater the need to eat it!

BLOAT

Gastric torsion, or bloat, is one of the more serious stomach disorders from which your Lurcher can suffer. The cause of this illness is still something of a mystery, although it is known to affect deep-chested dogs, usually at night after a large meal.

Bloat causes the stomach to swell with gas, hence the name. The digestive organs twist around inside the dog and cause severe pain. The twisting action of the stomach restricts the blood flow and oxygen intake of the dog, which can prove fatal. The

his ligaments or tendons rather than a muscle. Again, seek veterinary advice.

JOINT COMPLAINTS

Running dogs are particularly prone to complaints such as osteochondrosis (OCD) and osteoarthritis. A dog suffering from OCD has fractured bone cartilage. This breaks off from the humerus, in small pieces, and floats around the shoulder joint.

It is a condition which is caused by many different things but is normally only found in older dogs that have had injuries or repetitive strains in earlier life.

Regular health checks, usually every six months, will make early detection more likely, and the appropriate treatment can be given in good time.

With good care, your Lurcher should live a happy, healthy life.

condition can be further complicated if the dog develops shock.

A dog suffering from bloat will become restless, salivate to excess, and begin panting. His stomach may appear swollen and feel hard to the touch. If you think your dog has the condition, it is imperative that you get him to a vet as soon as possible, since the condition can be fatal if not caught in time.

Surgery is the only cure, as the vet has to place the stomach back in its original position. Time is of the essence, so it is advisable to leave for the veterinary practice straight away, while someone telephones the surgery to inform the vet of your dog's symptoms and to let them know of your impending arrival.

SKIN COMPLAINTS

Pressure sores and calluses, particularly on the elbows and hocks, are quite common in Lurchers because of the limited amount of fat between the skin and the bone. Sores occur when the dog lies down on hard surfaces for long periods of time.

The solution is to provide the dog with softer bedding and to apply dermatological moisturiser to the affected areas. Any sores should be seen by your vet, as they may ulcerate if left untreated.